Grandin

Pioneer for Animal Rights and Autism Awareness

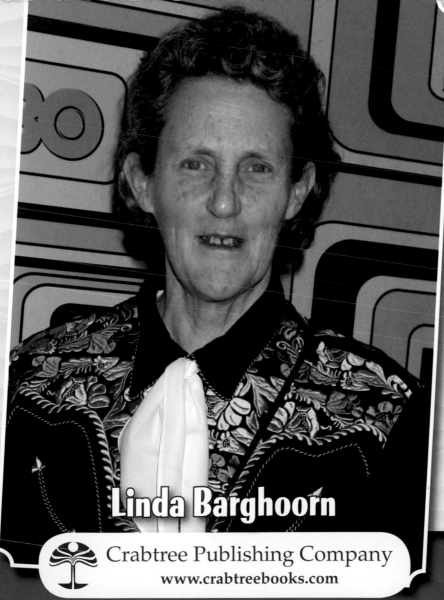

Linda Barghoorn

Crabtree Publishing Company
www.crabtreebooks.com

Author: Linda Barghoorn

Series research and development: Reagan Miller

Editorial director: Kathy Middleton

Editor: Crystal Sikkens

Proofreader: Janine Deschenes

Photo researchers: Samara Parent and Crystal Sikkens

Designer and prepress technician: Samara Parent

Print coordinator: Katherine Berti

Photographs:
AP Photo: ©The Denver Post, John Epperson: page 19

Bernd Foecking: page 16

Getty Images: ©Helen H. Richardson: pages 4-5; ©Jason Merritt: page 12; Portland Press Herald: page 17; © John Leyba: page 23; ©Michael Buckner: page 24; ©RJ Sangosti: page 25; ©Jerod Harris: page 26

Public Domain: page 9 (left), page 13, pages 20-21

Shutterstock.com: ©Helga Esteb: cover, title page, page 30; ©DutchScenery: page 11

Wikimedia Commons: ©mosso: page 18

All other images from Shutterstock

Library and Archives Canada Cataloguing in Publication

Barghoorn, Linda, author
    Temple Grandin : pioneer for animal rights and autism awareness / Linda Barghoorn.

(Remarkable lives revealed)
Includes index.
Issued in print and electronic formats.
ISBN 978-0-7787-2688-3 (hardback).--
ISBN 978-0-7787-2694-4 (paperback).--ISBN 978-1-4271-1809-7 (html)

    1. Grandin, Temple--Juvenile literature. 2. Autistic people--United States--Biography--Juvenile literature. 3. Animal scientists--United States--Biography--Juvenile literature. 4. Women animal specialists--United States--Biography--Juvenile literature. 5. Animal specialists--United States--Biography--Juvenile literature. 6. Animal welfare--United States--Juvenile literature. 7. Livestock--Handling--United States--Juvenile literature. I. Title.

RC553.A88B3654 2016   j616.85'8820092   C2016-904102-6
                                                   C2016-904103-4

Library of Congress Cataloging-in-Publication Data

Names: Barghoorn, Linda, author.
Title: Temple Grandin : pioneer for animal rights and autism awareness / Linda Barghoorn.
Description: St. Catharines, Ontario ; New York, New York : Crabtree Publishing Company, [2016] | Series: Remarkable lives revealed | Audience: Ages 7-10. | Audience: Grades 4 to 6. | Includes index.
Identifiers: LCCN 2016026655 (print) | LCCN 2016028159 (ebook) | ISBN 9780778726883 (reinforced library binding) | ISBN 9780778726944 (pbk.) | ISBN 9781427118097 (Electronic HTML)
Subjects: LCSH: Grandin, Temple--Juvenile literature. | Autistic people--United States--Biography--Juvenile literature. | Animal scientists--United States--Biography--Juvenile literature. | Women animal specialists--United States--Biography--Juvenile literature. | Animal specialists--United States--Biography--Juvenile literature. | Animal welfare--United States--Juvenile literature. | Livestock--Handling--United States--Juvenile literature.
Classification: LCC RC553.A88 B3654 2016 (print) | LCC RC553.A88 (ebook) | DDC 616.85/8820092 [B] --dc23
LC record available at https://lccn.loc.gov/2016026655

Crabtree Publishing Company
www.crabtreebooks.com   1-800-387-7650

Printed in Canada/082016/TL20160715

Published in Canada
Crabtree Publishing
616 Welland Ave.
St. Catharines, Ontario
L2M 5V6

Published in the United States
Crabtree Publishing
PMB 59051
350 Fifth Ave., 59th Floor
New York, NY 10118

Published in the United Kingdom
Crabtree Publishing
Maritime House
Basin Road North, Hove
BN41 1WR

Published in Australia
Crabtree Publishing
3 Charles Street
Coburg North
VIC, 3058

Contents

Never Give Up

Every person has a story to tell. These stories can inspire us to learn about others' lives. Some people are famous for their stories of bravery or courage. Other people may not be as well known, but can still have inspiring stories. Temple Grandin (*GRAHN-dihn*) is someone who is remarkable for her courage and determination. She was just four years old when she was **diagnosed** with autism. People thought she might never talk and go to school. But the only "never" Temple understood was "never give up." She refused to let autism limit her goals and dreams.

What is a Biography?

A biography is the story of a person's life and experiences. We read biographies with the purpose of learning about another person's life and thoughts. They can be based on many sources of information. Primary sources include a person's own words or pictures. Secondary sources include friends, family, media, and research.

Temple Grandin

Temple's Gift of Autism

Temple's tremendous courage helped her overcome the speech and behavior challenges that were part of her autism. She learned to talk, and then she grew up to become a famous professor, inventor, researcher, author, and speaker. She is strong, resourceful, and imaginative. With hard work and **perseverance**, she turned her diagnosis of autism into a remarkable gift.

As you read about Temple Grandin, think about the qualities that make her remarkable.

Learning about Autism

Autism is a brain **disorder** that affects the way a child's brain works. Scientists are working hard to learn more about autism. They still don't understand everything about what causes it and they believe there may be many different reasons. Children have autism from the time they are born. It is not a disease and is not **contagious**.

You can't catch autism from a classmate or friend.

Autism Spectrum

Autism describes a range of brain disorders. This is known as the autism **spectrum**. The autism spectrum includes many children that are affected in different ways. Some will never learn to talk. Others talk a lot. Some experience severe behavior problems and will always need help taking care of themselves. Others can grow up to lead independent lives and become brilliant inventors and artists. A child with autism may have a hard time speaking with people, making friends, or following instructions.

Children with autism are often very sensitive to sound, color, or light. This can make the world a confusing and frightening place for them.

Behaviors

Children with autism like to do many things that other children do, such as playing, reading, and art. In other ways, they are different. Their behavior can seem unusual because they are easily upset. They like things to always happen the same way. Change makes them anxious. They often have their own rules and feel everyone should follow them. Sometimes they are very **possessive** about a toy and they don't want to share. When they are upset they may use repetitive actions such as twirling, rolling, or rocking to calm themselves.

People with autism might find it hard to look at people, or to show their feelings with smiles or facial expressions.

Unique and Special

Every individual with autism is unique. Their minds let them see the world in different ways. Learning about how people with autism see the world can make our world a more interesting place for everyone. They should be encouraged to take pride in their special abilities and to develop them any way that they can.

The world needs all kinds of minds.

—Temple Grandin,
TED Talk, February 2010

Some people believe famous scientists and musicians such as Darwin (left) and Mozart (right) might have had autism. Back then, autism wasn't diagnosed.

Temple Grandin Growing Up

Mary Temple Grandin was born on August 29, 1947. She was the oldest of four children. She had two sisters and one brother. Her parents belonged to well-educated and wealthy families. Her mother was an actress and singer with a degree from Harvard University. Her father was a real estate agent and an **heir** to a large family business. Although Temple lived in a loving home, she faced many challenges of her own.

STATE STREET BANK

Temple was born in Boston, the capital and largest city in Massachusetts.

A Confusing World

As a child, Temple often behaved in a way that others thought was unusual. By the time she was four years old she still hadn't learned to talk. She disliked being hugged and touched. She was also very sensitive to unusual sounds. Because many things upset her she often had violent temper tantrums. She would voice her frustration with screams and peeping sounds. Temple found the world a very noisy, confusing, and scary place.

? THINK ABOUT IT

What were some of the unusual behaviors that suggested Temple was different?

Temple described her life with autism as if she was a ball bouncing through a noisy, bright pinball machine.

Diagnosis

Temple's mother was concerned about her daughter's behavior and took her to a brain specialist. Temple was diagnosed with autism in 1951 when she was four years old. Her doctor and father felt she should be put in an **institution** away from society. But Temple's mother refused. She insisted that Temple would stay with their family and go to school like a normal child.

Temple's mother Eustacia Cutler has always believed in her. Because of this, they have always had a close relationship.

Autism Misunderstood

Autism had only been identified for the first time in 1944. This was just several years before Temple was diagnosed. At the time, doctors thought it was a form of brain damage. They didn't know how to treat it. People didn't understand autism, and were embarrassed and afraid of people that had it. Children with autism were often hidden away and **isolated** from society. They were not allowed to share life with their families, play with other children, or take part in school. Few were given opportunities to lead productive lives. They often grew up to be very withdrawn, sad, and alone.

Leo Kanner was the first doctor to begin using the term autism to describe children that were highly intelligent, or smart, but had some behavioral and social problems.

Speech Therapy

Temple's mother was not afraid of autism. She was determined to help Temple lead a happy, full life. She hired a speech **therapist** and placed Temple in a strict program of speech therapy lessons. These lessons taught Temple how to speak slowly, make proper sentences, and listen to what others were saying. Temple spent many hours each week practicing speaking and listening skills. This took a lot of determination, patience, and perseverance.

What is a Speech Therapist?

Speech therapists help people with speaking and language disorders learn to put words and sounds together to communicate.

Social Skills and Independence

Temple's mother also pushed her to be independent. Manners and rules were very important when Temple was growing up. Children were expected to learn to share, take turns, greet people politely, and say "please" and "thank you." She learned about the value of money and how to go shopping. She was encouraged to work and play with other children. Rules helped organize the world for Temple. They helped her see patterns in the way people behaved that she could copy.

" When I was 8 years old, my mother made me be a party hostess—shake hands, take coats.

—Temple Grandin, www.templegrandin.com "

? THINK ABOUT IT

Why were Temple's childhood rules and expectations so important?

Turning Autism into a Gift

Even though she worked hard to fit in, Temple was still considered different by many classmates at school. Her speech and movements were often awkward. As a teenager, she was often teased and bullied. This made her feel very nervous and insecure. She was expelled, or forced to leave, her junior high school when she was 14 because she threw a book at a girl who teased her. Temple had to learn how to properly deal with people who didn't understand why she was different.

Finding her Strengths

Hampshire Country School is a special high school where teachers work closely with students with special needs. The teachers helped Temple develop her unique talents and skills. She had difficulty with math, but liked science and solving puzzles. She was encouraged to explore her love of art and drawing. Drawing helped her develop her skill as a visual thinker. A visual thinker is someone who thinks in pictures instead of words.

Temple translates words into a series of pictures in her mind like a video. This helps her understand information and solve problems in a distinctive way.

> " *I think in pictures. Pictures is my first language. English is my second language.*
>
> **—Temple Grandin, Stairway to Heaven, 2009** "

Temple decribes what it's like to be a visual thinker in her book Thinking in Pictures.

"I hardly know what to say about this remarkable book.... It provides a way to understand the many kinds of sentience, human and animal, that adorn the earth."
— Elizabeth Marshall Thomas, author of The Hidden Life of Dogs

THINKING IN PICTURES

AND OTHER REPORTS FROM WITH AUTISM

A Science Teacher

Temple's high school science teacher, Mr. Carlock, was an important person in her life. He recognized her talent for science and her eagerness to discover new ideas. He gave her different problems to solve. One of them was to try and figure out how an **optical illusion** room worked, and then design a similar room. Temple became obsessed with trying to solve this problem, until one day she finally did. Problems like this inspired her love of science and helped build her self-confidence.

? THINK ABOUT IT

What role did Mr. Carlock play in Temple's life?

An optical illusion room makes one person appear taller than another person located in a different corner of the room.

The Woman who Thinks like a Cow

Temple adored animals. In high school she rode horses. She also took care of them, cleaned their stalls, and fed them. When she was sixteen, Temple was invited to her aunt's ranch. She began to understand that cows and people with autism often react to the world around them in similar ways. Sights and sounds that are new or unusual can frighten them. Temple felt like she could see the world through the animals' eyes.

An Activist for Animals

Temple worked often with the cows on her aunt's ranch. She noticed that cows were calmer when they were inside the squeeze chute, a machine that held them still while they were being given shots or marked with a brand. She was curious to understand how it would feel, so she climbed inside. It wasn't very comfortable, but it helped her relax just like the cows. With Mr. Carlock's help, Temple built her first squeeze machine for people who are uncomfortable being touched. At age 18, this marked the beginning of her science career.

Temple's Squeeze Machine

A person steps into the box and lies down. The machine makes you feel relaxed, like you are being hugged gently.

Improving Animals' Lives

Temple graduated from high school and went on to earn a Masters and PhD in Animal Science. Her ability to "think like a cow" helps her understand how animals see and feel. She has used this knowledge to build a unique career specializing in **animal welfare** and designing **humane** equipment for handling **livestock**. She wants to improve the lives of animals that are raised for food. Her understanding and **compassion** for animals helped Temple design the buildings and equipment that handle half the livestock raised in North America.

Cattle-squeeze chutes, such as this one, are what inspired Temple's hug machine.

Ethics versus Food

Some people believe we should stop using animals for food. Temple believes we should treat the animals we raise for food in an **ethical** way. She understands animals feel emotion and pain. Through her studies she has developed better methods for the treatment of animals. She consults with fast-food companies such as McDonalds and Burger King to put these ideas in place.

? THINK ABOUT IT

Do you agree with Temple that we owe animals respect as we raise them for food? Why?

Temple's **ingenuity** and persistence have led to the more ethical treatment of animals raised for food across North America.

Professor and Researcher

Temple is considered the world's leading expert on livestock welfare. She works as a Professor of Animal Science at Colorado State University. Her dedication to animal science has influenced hundreds of her university students. They are continuing her work to improve the lives of animals being raised for food. Temple also works as a researcher and travels the world to speak about animal welfare.

> *I think using animals for food is an ethical thing to do, but we've got to do it right…We owe the animal respect.*
>
> **—Temple Grandin,**
> **Euthanasia and the Slaughter of**
> **Livestock, 1994**

Temple has written three books about animal welfare, including the book entitled Humane Livestock Handling.

An Activist for Autism

Temple's life was also featured in a movie with Clare Danes called Temple Grandin.

Temple began speaking publicly about her experiences with autism in the 1980s. She has delivered hundreds of speeches in different countries. She works tirelessly to advance the rights of people with autism. She has been interviewed on many television shows, including *20/20* and *60 Minutes*, and on CNN. In 2010, *TIME* magazine named her on its list of "The 100 Most Influential People in the World."

Asperger Syndrome

When Temple grew up, doctors decided she had Asperger syndrome. Asperger syndrome is a type of autism. People with Asperger's may have some symptoms of autism, but they are often very intelligent and can learn about many different things. Temple Grandin has many talents, but she is especially gifted in science and has a unique understanding of animals. Her achievements have taught us not to underestimate the ability of people with autism and Asperger syndrome. She has worked hard to overcome the label of autism.

> " See the person, not the label.
>
> —Temple Grandin,
> The Way I See it: A Personal Look at
> Autism & Asperger's, 2011

Temple, shown here at Colorado State University, speaks to parents, teachers, and autism experts about how they can meet the needs of college students with autism and help them succeed.

A Source of Inspiration

Temple speaks about her life with courage and honesty. She has had to conquer many obstacles. She has been guided by hope, determination, and discovery. Her achievements have made her an extraordinary source of inspiration for people with autism and their families. As an author and scientist, Temple has challenged society's attitudes about autism. She has written seven books on autism, including *The Way I See It* and *The Autistic Brain*. She has helped **empower** people with autism to pursue productive and rewarding lives.

Temple signs autographs for fans after discussing her new book Emergence: Labeled Autistic.

Attitudes Today

We have learned a lot about how to treat people with autism since it was first discovered. Autistic people have the right to participate like everyone else and be encouraged to reach their full **potential**. Temple believes every person with autism should have access to special education programs and speech therapy at an early age. She knows this is important to give them the best chance to have successful lives as adults and to contribute to the world in a meaningful way.

Today, everyone understands that people who have autism have the right to education just like everyone else.

A Voice for Others

The little girl with no voice has made an incredible journey. Today, Temple Grandin is the most accomplished and respected person with autism in the world. She is a strong voice for others with autism who can't always speak for themselves. She encourages teachers, classmates, friends, and families to help children who have autism reach their full potential by being patient, understanding, and supportive.

> I had people in my life who didn't give up on me: my mother, my aunt, my science teacher.
>
> —Temple Grandin,
> Different not Less, 2012.

How to be a Friend to Someone with Autism:

- Invite them to play with you and your friends.

- Don't tease them if they act differently.

- Be patient if they don't understand.

- Accept their differences.

- Understand that they have talents and intelligence, but just in a different way.

- Protect them from things that upset them.

- Help other kids learn about autism.

Writing Prompts

1. Based on what you've learned about Temple Grandin, have your attitudes and ideas about people who have autism changed? How?

2. Temple Grandin is an important role model—especially for people who have autism. What are some of her qualities that might inspire others to reach their potential?

3. Which people were important in Temple's life? How did they help her achieve success as an adult?

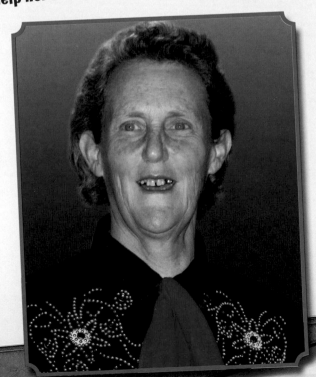

Learning More

Books

Temple Grandin: How the Girl Who Loved Cows Embraced Autism and Changed the World. HMH Books for Young Readers. Sy Montgomery and Temple Grandin. 2012.

Different Like Me: My Book of Autism Heroes. Jennifer Elder. Jessica Kingsley Publishers. 2005

The Autism Acceptance Book. Ellen Sabin. Watering Can. 2006.

Autism Spectrum Disorder. Marguerite Rodger. Crabtree Publishing Company. 2014

Cory Stories: A Kid's Book About Living With ADHD. Jeanne Kraus. Magination Press. 2004.

Looking after Louis. Lesley Ely, Albert Whitman and Company. 2004.

Websites

www.templegrandin.com
Temple Grandin's official website. Learn more about Temple, her featured autism articles, info on her books and dvds, and her upcoming conferences.

www.bridges4kids.org/pdf/Growing_Up_Booklet.pdf
Autism Society of America. Discusses how children with autism behave and how to be their friend.

www.cdc.gov/ncbddd/kids/autism.html
A Kid's Site for learning about Autism, from the National Center on Birth Defects and Developmental Disabilities.

http://kidshealth.org/en/kids/autism.html
KidsHealth, The Nemours Foundation. Explains autism, what causes it and how to help children with autism

www.cyh.com/HealthTopics/HealthTopicDetailsKids.aspx?p=335&np=287&id=2339#5
Women and Children's Health Network. What is Asperger syndrome

Glossary

activist Someone who helps make changes in society

animal welfare The everyday care and well-being of animals

compassion Caring deeply for something

contagious Describing something easily spread from one person to another

diagnose To determine the identity of a disease or disorder

disorder A physical or mental illness

empower To enable someone to do something

ethical Something that is honest and morally right

heir Someone who will receive someone else's property when they die

humane Gentle or kind

ingenuity A skill allowing someone to solve a problem or invent something

institution A hospital for people who have mental or physical disabilities

isolated Separate from others

livestock Cows, pigs, sheep, or other animals raised on a farm or ranch

optical illusion Something that appears different than it is; a trick of the eye

perseverance Not giving up

possessive Describing someone that wishes to have control over their belongings

potential Qualities or abilities that may be developed which lead to success

spectrum A range or scale of something

therapist Someone who provides treatment to cure an injury or disease

Index